Nn Oo Pp

Qq Rr

Ss Tt Uu

Vv Ww

Xx Yy Zz

This book belongs to:

....

....

....

Written by Sue Graves
Illustrated by Ruth Galloway (Advocate),
Emma Lake (Advocate) and Kim Blundell

Language consultant: Betty Root

This is a Parragon Publishing book
This edition published in 2004

Parragon Publishing
Queen Street House
4 Queen Street
BATH, BA1 1HE, UK

Copyright © Parragon 2004
ISBN 1-40543-262-4

Printed in China

My Picture Dictionary

p

Contents

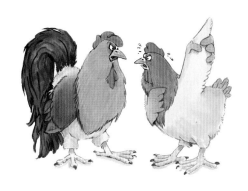

About My Picture Dictionary

Using a dictionary requires several different skills, from identifying the letters in a word to recognizing the order of words in the alphabet. **My Picture Dictionary** is designed to help your child develop alphabetical skills. This dictionary can be used together with any of the **First Readers** books or on its own.

Each headword has a picture clue to help children predict the word and its meaning. Any difficult or irregular plurals of nouns are given, as well as the past tense of each verb. Each headword has a simple, clear definition, plus a sample sentence that uses the word in context.

the headword ➤ **apple**
An apple is a round fruit. ◄ the definition
Apples can be green, red, or yellow.

the picture ➤

This apple has a red, shiny skin. ◄ the sample sentence

Helping your child

In order that your child gains the most benefit from using this **First Readers** dictionary, the following suggestions may be useful:

- Explain that a dictionary gives the meaning of words.
- Point out the alphabet strip across the top of each page.
- Help your child to find an entry by looking for the initial letter of the word.
- Now explain that because several words begin with the same letter, you need to look at the next and following letters to find the word.
- Once the word has been found, look at the picture first. Then, help your child to read the definition.
- Last of all, read the accompanying sample sentence together.
- You can use the sentences as a starting point for talking about the characters and the stories in which they appear.

add (added)

When you add, you put things together to make more.

Jack adds the beans in his hand.

airplane

An airplane is a machine that can fly. It has two wings and a tail.

You can travel by airplane to faraway places.

address

Your address is the name of a house, a street, and a town or city.

You write an address on an envelope.

Daddy Bear
The Cottage
Forest Lane
BEARTOWN

alphabet

The alphabet is all the letters from a to z. You use the letters of the alphabet to make words.

Do you know all 26 letters of the alphabet?

animal

An animal is a living thing that can breathe and move.

The ugly duckling saw lots of animals on the farm.

arm

Your arm is the part of your body between your shoulder and your hand.

Goldilocks waves her arm.

apple

An apple is a round fruit. Apples can be green, red, or yellow.

This apple has a red, shiny skin.

arrow

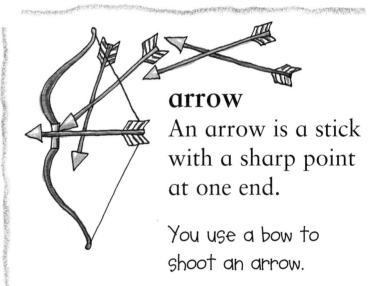

An arrow is a stick with a sharp point at one end.

You use a bow to shoot an arrow.

apron

An apron is a piece of cloth. You wear an apron to keep your clothes clean.

Mommy Bear wears an apron when she cooks.

ask (asked)

You ask a question when you want to find something out.

"Will you take this basket to your grandma?" asks Mommy.

baby (babies)

A baby is a very young child or animal.

Sleeping Beauty was a very beautiful baby.

bag

You can carry things in a bag. Bags can be made of plastic, cloth, or leather.

What do you think is inside this bag?

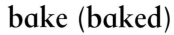

bake (baked)

To bake means to cook food in an oven.

The old woman baked a gingerbread man.

ball

A ball is a round or egg-shaped object. You throw, kick, or catch a ball.

What do you play with each of these balls?

A ball is also a special kind of party where people dance.

Prince Charming met Cinderella at the ball.

balloon

A balloon is a thin, rubber bag. You fill it with air or water.

You blow air into a balloon to make it bigger.

barn

A barn is a big building on a farm. Animals often sleep inside a barn at night.

The barn had a big, red door.

basket

You carry things inside a basket. A basket can be made of thin strips of wood or metal.

Red Riding Hood had food in her basket.

bean

A bean is a seed that you can eat. Beans grow on a tall plant called a beanstalk.

Jack had five magic beans.

bear

A bear is a large, furry animal.

Here are Daddy Bear, Mommy Bear, and Baby Bear.

bed

A bed is a place where you lie down. You can rest or go to sleep in a bed.

Goldilocks went to sleep in Baby Bear's bed.

beast

A beast is a wild animal.

The Beast was big and ugly.

bee

A bee is a small animal with wings. Some bees make honey.

Bees make a buzzing noise when they fly.

beautiful

Beautiful is being pretty to look at.

Beauty was a beautiful girl.

bicycle

A bicycle has two wheels. You can ride a bicycle.

Can you ride a bicycle like this one?

big

Big is the same as large. Something that is big is not small.

Big Billy Goat Gruff was the biggest goat.

bite (bit)

When you bite something, you cut into it with your teeth.

The boy started to bite the apple.

bird

A bird is an animal with two wings and feathers. Most birds can fly.

Birds are many different sizes and colors.

blind

If you are blind you cannot see.

This blind woman has a special guide dog to help her find her way.

birthday

Your birthday is the day you were born. You may have a party each year on the day of your birthday.

How old will you be on your next birthday?

blow (blew)

You push air out of your mouth when you blow.

The wolf blew down the house of straw.

book

A book has pages made of paper. There may be words or pictures in a book. You read stories in some books.

Which is your favorite book?

bread

Bread is a food made from flour and water. You bake bread in an oven.

You use bread to make sandwiches and toast.

bottle

You can put water, milk, or other liquids in a bottle. Bottles are made of glass or plastic.

Babies drink milk from bottles like these.

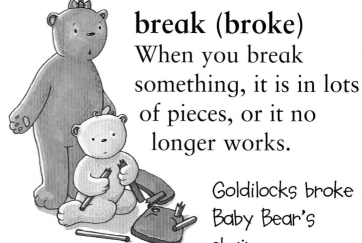

break (broke)

When you break something, it is in lots of pieces, or it no longer works.

Goldilocks broke Baby Bear's chair.

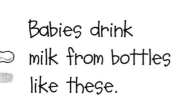

bowl

A bowl is a deep, round dish. You eat foods such as cereal and soup from a bowl.

Goldilocks found three bowls.

brick

A brick is a small, hard block. You can build a house with bricks.

Bricks are made of baked mud or clay.

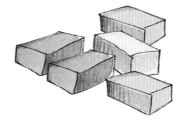

bridge

A bridge goes over a river, a road, or a railway. You cross a bridge to get to the other side.

The car drives over the bridge.

build (built)

You build something by putting lots of parts together.

"I'll build my house with bricks," said the third little pig.

broom

A broom is a big brush with a long handle. You sweep a floor with a broom.

Snow White swept the floor with her broom.

bus

A bus is a big vehicle. It carries people from place to place.

Do you go to school by bus?

brush (brushed)

When you brush your hair, you make it neat.

Snow White brushed her long hair.

butterfly (butterflies)

A butterfly is an insect with four big wings. Many butterflies are very colorful.

Look for a butterfly in the garden in summer!

cake

A cake is a sweet food that is baked in an oven. It is made of flour, eggs, sugar, and butter.

Which kind of cake do you like best?

cap

A cap is a small hat.

The cap flew off the wolf's head.

cage

A cage is a box or a room with bars around it.

The witch locked Hansel in a cage.

cape

A cape is a long coat with no sleeves. You wrap it around your body.

Little Red Riding Hood had a red cape.

car

A car has four wheels and an engine. It can take people for rides.

It's fun to help wash the car.

cat

A cat is a furry animal with sharp claws. People often keep cats as pets.

This cat has white fur on its front.

card

A card is a piece of stiff paper. It can have a picture or words on it.

You send a card to people on their birthdays.

catch (caught)

When you catch something, you take hold of it with your hands.

Can you catch a ball?

castle

A castle is a big building with thick walls made of stone.

A giant lived in the castle.

cave

A cave is a hole in the side of a hill. It can also be a hole under the ground.

The fox's den was in a cave.

chair

You sit on a chair. A chair has a seat and a back.

Goldilocks sat in the middle-sized chair.

child (children)

A child is a young boy or girl.

The children wanted to play with the ugly duckling.

cherry (cherries)

A cherry is a small, red fruit. It has a tiny pit in the middle.

Do you like to eat cherries?

chimney

A chimney is built on top of a building. It lets out smoke from a fire inside.

The big, bad wolf climbed into the chimney.

chicken

A chicken is a bird that lives on farms. Some chickens lay eggs.

Chicken-Licken was a lucky chicken!

chin

Your chin is the bottom part of your face below your mouth.

The witch had a pointed chin.

chop (chopped)

When you chop something, you cut it into smaller pieces.

The woodcutter chopped the wood with his ax.

clock

A clock is a machine that tells you the time.

The time on this clock is a quarter past twelve.

clever

Someone who can understand or do things very well is clever.

Clever people usually work very hard.

clothes

You put clothes on your body to keep you warm.

Clothes are things like pants, jackets, and socks.

climb (climbed)

When you climb something, you go up it.

The prince climbed up Rapunzel's hair.

cloud

A cloud floats in the sky. It appears white or gray.

The beanstalk went up into the clouds.

coach (coaches)

A coach is a vehicle with wheels. It is pulled by horses.

A pumpkin was turned into a coach for Cinderella.

cottage

A cottage is a small house in the country or near the sea.

The three bears lived in a cottage.

cold

When it is cold, it is not hot.

When it is cold, you wear lots of clothes to keep warm.

count (counted)

When you count things, you use numbers to say how many there are.

Do you use your fingers to help you count?

cook (cooked)

When you cook food, you heat it before you eat it.

Mommy Bear liked to cook porridge.

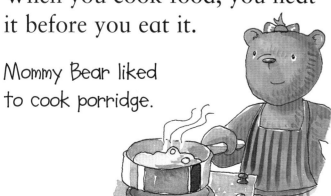

cow

A cow is a farm animal. Cows give us milk.

The cow wanted to eat the gingerbread man.

crack (cracked)

When something cracks it breaks open, often with a loud noise.

The egg cracked open.

cry (cried)

When you cry, tears fall from your eyes.

The little girl was sad, and she began to cry.

creep (crept)

If you creep, you move quietly and slowly.

Jack took the hen and crept away.

cupboard

A cupboard is a small closet with shelves. You keep things inside it.

Do you keep your toys in a cupboard?

cross

If you are cross, you are angry.

Rumpelstiltskin was very cross.

cut (cut)

When you cut something, you use scissors or a knife.

The witch cut off Rapunzel's hair.

D d

dance (danced)
To dance is to move in time to music.

Do you like to dance?

dark
When it is dark, there is no light.

Hansel and Gretel were lost in a dark wood.

deer
A deer is an animal that can run fast. Some deer have big horns on their heads.

A baby deer has white spots.

desk

A desk is a table where you can write and work.

You can sit at a desk like this to do your homework.

doctor

A doctor helps sick people to get better.

The doctor looked at the boy's red spots.

dig (dug)

When you dig, you make a hole in the ground.

Dad likes to dig in the garden.

dog

A dog is an animal that barks and has four legs. Some dogs work on farms, and some are pets.

The dog barked at the ugly duckling.

dinosaur

A dinosaur is an animal that lived a long, long time ago. There are no dinosaurs alive today.

Some dinosaurs were taller than trees.

doll

A doll is a toy that looks like a small child or a baby.

This doll wears a pretty dress.

donkey

A donkey is an animal with long ears. It looks like a small horse.

The donkey is eating the turnip leaves.

down

When you go down, you move from a high place to a low place.

Jack climbed down the beanstalk.

door

A door opens and shuts. It can be the way into a room, a house, or a closet.

The wolf knocked on the door.

dragon

A dragon is a make-believe animal from story books. Many dragons breathe out fire.

This dragon breathes out fire and smoke.

dove

A dove is a bird that makes a cooing sound.

Snow White fed the doves each day.

dream

A dream is the pictures you see and the sounds you hear when you are asleep.

Do you remember your dreams when you wake up?

dress (dresses)

A dress looks like a top and a skirt that are joined together. Girls and women wear dresses.

Beauty's sister wanted a new dress.

drum

A drum is a musical instrument. It makes a noise when you hit it.

You can use two sticks to bang on a drum.

drink (drank)

To drink is to swallow a liquid such as water.

Goldilocks drank the milk from Baby Bear's cup.

duck

A duck is a bird that can swim and fly.

The mother duck sat on the eggs in her nest.

drop (dropped)

To drop something is to let it fall.

Hansel dropped the pebbles on the ground.

dwarf (dwarfs)

A dwarf is a very small person.

The dwarfs waved goodbye to Snow White.

eat (ate)
When you eat, you put food in your mouth and then swallow it.

The goat likes to eat grass.

egg
Some animals lay eggs. Baby animals can hatch from eggs.

The mother duck laid four eggs.

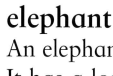

ear
You hear with your ears. Your ears are on the side of your head.

The wolf had very big ears.

elephant
An elephant is a very big animal. It has a long trunk and two tusks.

An elephant sprays water through its long trunk.

elf (elves)

An elf is a small person who is found in fairy tales. Elves are often quite naughty.

The elves made perfect shoes.

enormous

If something is enormous, it is very big.

The turnip was enormous!

emperor

An emperor is in charge of a group of countries called an empire. He is like a king.

The Emperor wanted a new suit.

evening

The evening is the early part of the night.

You get ready for bed in the evening.

end

The end of something is the last part of it.

Jack cut the end of the beanstalk.

eye

You see with your eyes. You have two eyes in the front of your head.

The troll had very big eyes.

F f

fall (fell)

To fall is to drop down.

The troll fell into the water.

family (families)

A family is a group of people who are related to each other.

This family has a grandparent, parents, and children.

fairy (fairies)

A fairy is a make-believe person with wings. You read about fairies in fairy tales.

The fairy waved her magic wand.

farm

A farm is a place where a farmer looks after animals or grows food crops.

There are lots of animals on this farm.

farmer

A farmer is a person who takes care of a farm.

The farmer called out to the gingerbread man.

father

A father is a man who has a child or children.

Beauty's father had three daughters.

fast

Fast means the same as quick. To go fast is to move quickly.

If you run fast, you can win the race.

feather

A feather is very light and fluffy. A bird has feathers on its body.

Some ducks have green, brown, and white feathers.

fat

A fat person or animal is big and heavy.

If the monster eats all the time, it will grow fat.

field

A field is a piece of land in the country. Grass grows in fields.

The tractor is in the field.

finger

A finger is part of your hand. Each hand has four fingers and a thumb.

The princess pricked her finger.

first

The first comes before all the others. The first number is number 1.

Mary came in first and won a big cup.

fire

You make fire when you burn something. Fire is very hot.

You can burn wood to make a fire.

fish (fish)

A fish is an animal that lives in water. A fish has fins and a tail to help it swim.

The fish jumped out of the water.

fire truck

A fire truck helps to put out fires. It carries people and all the things needed to put out a fire.

The fire truck has a very big ladder.

fit (fit)

Something fits you when it is the right shape and size for you.

The shoe fit Cinderella's foot.

flap (flapped)

When you flap something, you move it up and down.

The ugly duckling flapped his wings.

fly (flew)

To fly is to move through the air.

The rocket will fly to the moon.

floor

The floor is the bottom of a room. You walk on the floor.

Rumpelstiltskin fell through the floor.

follow (followed)

To follow is to go behind something or to go the same way.

Hansel and Gretel followed the pebbles.

flower

A flower is part of a plant or tree. Many flowers come in bright colors.

Little Red Riding Hood picked the flowers.

food

Apples, bread, cheese, and chicken are different kinds of food. You eat food to grow and to stay healthy.

Which of these foods do you like to eat?

foot (feet)

Your foot is at the end of your leg. You walk on your two feet.

How big are your feet?

fork

A fork has pointed parts. You use a small fork to pick up food. You use a big fork to dig in the garden.

It's hard to eat peas with a fork!

forest

A forest is a large wood.

There are lots of trees in a forest.

fox (foxes)

A fox is a wild animal with a bushy tail.

Foxy-Loxy was a clever fox.

forget (forgot)

If you forget, you do not remember to do something.

Mom always forgets to bring the umbrella.

friend

A friend is someone you like and who likes you as well.

Friends play together at playtime.

frighten (frightened)

To frighten someone is to make them feel afraid of someone or something.

The witch frightened Hansel and Gretel.

fruit

A fruit is a part of a tree or a plant. You can eat many kinds of fruit.

Which of these fruits do you like to eat?

frog

A frog is a small animal. It can live on land and in water. Frogs can jump up high.

A frog has two very long back legs.

full

If something is full, there is no room for anything else.

The wolf's tummy was very full.

front

The front of something is the part that you see first.

Two horses stood at the front of the coach.

funny

When something is funny, it makes you laugh.

My brother makes very funny faces.

game

You can play a game for fun. Most games have rules that you follow.

Do you play games on your computer?

gate

A gate is a door in a fence, a hedge, or a wall.

Goldilocks opened the gate.

garden

A garden is on land around a house. Trees and other plants grow in gardens.

Beauty picked the roses in the Beast's garden.

giant

A giant is a very big person. You read about giants in fairy tales.

The giant was a huge man.

gingerbread

Gingerbread is a cake or a cookie that is made with a spice called ginger.

The gingerbread man jumped out.

glasses

People wear glasses to help them see better. Glasses are made from glass or plastic.

The little old woman wore glasses.

giraffe

A giraffe is a very tall animal that lives in Africa. It has a long neck and long legs.

Giraffes can eat the leaves at the tops of trees.

glove

A glove is a covering for your hand. Gloves keep your hands warm.

The prince wore white gloves.

give (gave)

When you give, you let another person have something.

Little Red Riding Hood gave the flowers to the wolf.

goat

A goat is an animal with horns. A male goat also has a beard.

There were three Billy Goats Gruff.

godmother

A godmother makes special promises to look after a child.

The fairy godmother waved her magic wand.

goose (geese)

A goose is a big bird with a long neck. A goose can swim and fly.

Goosey-Loosey was a white goose.

gold

Gold is a shiny, yellow metal. Gold is very expensive.

The thieves wanted thread made from gold.

gown

A gown is a long dress. You wear a gown at a party or a ball.

The fairy godmother turned Cinderella's dress into a ball gown.

good

When you are good, you behave well. You are also good if you are kind.

Hansel was a good brother.

grape

A grape is a small fruit. Grapes grow in groups called bunches.

Grapes grow on a plant called a vine.

grass

Grass is a plant with thin, green leaves. You need lots of grass to make a lawn.

Cows and sheep like to eat grass.

grow (grew)

When something grows, it gets bigger and bigger.

You grow a little taller each year.

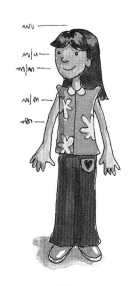

greedy

You are greedy if you want more than you need.

The monster was very greedy.

guitar

A guitar is a musical instrument. It has six strings and a long handle.

Have you ever played a guitar?

ground

The ground is the earth that you walk on. Plants grow in the ground.

The enormous turnip grew in the ground.

gulp (gulped)

When you gulp, you swallow quickly.

The fox gulped the gingerbread man.

H h

hammer

You use a hammer to hit nails into wood and other materials.

The elf hit the nail with his hammer.

hand

Your hands are at the end of your arms. You have four fingers and a thumb at the end of each hand.

You wave with your hands.

hair

Hair is soft and fine. It grows on the head or body of people and other animals.

Goldilocks had golden hair.

handsome

A handsome person is someone who is good-looking.

The Beast turned into a handsome prince.

happy

When you are happy you are pleased.

Rapunzel and the prince were very happy.

head

Your head is the part of your body where your ears, eyes, nose, and mouth are. It is on top of your neck.

Your hair grows on top of your head.

hard

Something that is hard is not soft to touch.

Daddy Bear's bed was too hard.

hear (heard)

To hear is to get sounds through your ears.

The girl heard the cat's loud noise.

hatch (hatched)

When animals hatch, they come out of eggs. Chicks, ducklings, and baby crocodiles all hatch.

The duckling hatched out of its egg.

heavy

Something that is heavy may be hard to pick up or carry.

A sack of potatoes is very heavy.

hen

A hen is a bird that lays eggs. Hens are female chickens.

The hen had a bright orange beak.

hill

A hill is higher than the land around it. It is a little mountain.

It is hard work to walk up a hill.

hide (hid)

To hide is to go where no one can see you or find you.

The shoemaker and his wife hid in the workshop.

honey

Honey is a sweet, sticky food that is made by bees.

You can spread honey on your bread.

high

If something is high, it is above other things. It can be hard to reach high places.

Daddy Bear's chair was too high.

hood

You wear a hood over your head. It can be part of a coat, a cape, or a jacket.

Little Red Riding Hood's cape had a hood.

hoof (hooves)

A hoof is the very hard part of the foot of some animals. Horses, cows, and goats have hooves.

The little Billy Goat Gruff's hooves went trip trap over the bridge.

hot

When something is hot, it is very warm.

The porridge was too hot to eat.

horn

A horn is a hard, pointed part on the head of some animals. Deer and goats have two horns.

A rhinoceros has one very big horn.

house

A house is a building where people can live.

The witch's house was made of candy and cake.

horse

A horse is a big, strong animal. People like to ride horses.

The horse had a long gray tail.

hungry

When you are hungry, you want to eat food.

Hansel and Gretel were very hungry.

ice

Ice is water that has frozen.
Ice is very hard and cold.

This piece of ice is
an ice cube.

idea

An idea is
something that
you think of.

You need a good idea
when you write a
new story.

ice cream

Ice cream is a
creamy, frozen
food.

Do you like to
eat ice cream?

ill

When you are ill,
you are not well.

Grandma was ill,
so she went
to bed.

ink

Ink is a colored liquid. You use ink when you write with a pen.

Do you ever write with a pen and ink?

invite (invited)

If you invite someone, you ask the person to come to something such as a party.

The prince invited every girl in the land to a ball.

insect

An insect is a little creature, such as a bee, a ladybug, or a butterfly. Insects have six legs.

You can find lots of insects in a garden.

island

An island is some land that has water all around it.

The king's castle was on an island.

inside

To be inside something is to be in it.

Snow White lay inside a glass box.

ivy (ivies)

Ivy is a climbing plant. It has shiny leaves.

Ivy often climbs up the walls of houses.

jar

A jar is a holder made of glass or plastic. You can keep jelly or honey inside a jar.

The shoemaker kept nails in a jar.

jaw

Your jaw is one of the bones that hold your teeth. It is the bottom part of your face.

This shark has very big jaws.

jack-in-the-box

A jack-in-the-box is a toy that jumps up from inside a box.

A jack-in-the-box jumps up when you lift its lid.

jewel

A jewel is a beautiful stone that costs a lot of money. A diamond is one kind of jewel.

There were jewels in the crowns of the king and queen.

jigsaw

A jigsaw is a picture that has been cut into shapes. You put the shapes together to make the picture.

You can do a very big jigsaw on the floor.

juice

Juice is a liquid that comes out of fruit if you squeeze it.

Do you like to drink orange juice?

jolly

If you are jolly, you feel very happy.

The tiny elf was very jolly.

jump (jumped)

To jump is to leap up quickly into the air.

The gingerbread man jumped onto the fox's nose.

juggler

A juggler can throw and catch lots of things at the same time.

You can watch jugglers at a circus.

jungle

A jungle is a thick forest in very hot, rainy parts of the world.

Tigers, monkeys, and snakes live in the jungle.

kettle

You boil water in a kettle. A kettle has a handle and a spout.

You use this kind of kettle on a stove.

kick (kicked)

When you kick something, you hit it hard with your foot.

The boy kicked the soccer ball into the air.

key

A key is a special shape of metal. You fit a key into a lock.

You turn a key in a lock to open a door.

kind

A person who is kind likes to help other people.

Beauty tried to be kind to the Beast.

king

A king is a person who has been born to be the head of a country.

A king sometimes wears a crown.

kitten

A kitten is a young cat.

This cat has five kittens.

kiss (kissed)

To kiss is to touch with the lips.

The prince wanted to kiss Snow White.

knife (knives)

A knife has a long, sharp edge to cut things.

You use a big knife to cut bread.

kite

A kite is a toy that flies. Wind lifts the kite into the air. A kite has a long string.

It's best to fly a kite on a windy day.

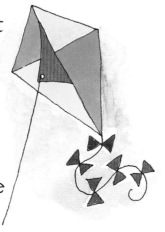

knot

A knot is where two ends of string or material are tied together.

The scarf was tied in a big knot.

ladder

A ladder is a set of steps that you move. You climb a ladder to reach a high place.

The little pig climbed the ladder.

lamp

A lamp gives you light where you need it.

Do you have a lamp by your bed?

lake

A lake is an area of water with land all around it.

Plants grow at the edge of the lake.

last

The last is the end one. It comes after all the others.

Baby Bear was the last one to walk past.

laugh

You laugh when you think something is funny.

Everyone began to laugh at the Emperor.

left

Left is the opposite side of right.

Foxy-Loxy is on the left. Chicken-Licken is on the right.

leaf (leaves)

A leaf is the flat, green part of a plant.

Leaves are many different shapes.

leg

Your leg is a long part of your body. You stand and walk on your legs.

A cow has four long legs.

leather

Leather is the skin of dead animals. You make shoes and bags out of leather.

The shoemaker cut out the leather.

lettuce

A lettuce is a vegetable with big, green leaves.

You eat lettuce in a salad.

lie (lay)

If you lie down, you rest your body flat on something.

Goldilocks went to lie on the tiny, little bed.

little

Little means not at all big. Little is the same as small.

The little Billy Goat Gruff was very small.

like

If you like something or somebody, you are pleased with the person or the thing.

The children like to eat spaghetti.

lock (locked)

When you lock something, you close it with a key.

You can lock this secret diary.

list

A list is a group of names written down one under the other.

Dan
Tom
Peter
David
Snozbert
Shorty
Adam
Will
Dizzy

The Queen made a list of names.

locket

A locket is a tiny case that you hang around your neck. A locket holds something special.

This locket has a picture inside it.

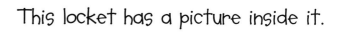

long

Something that is long is not short.

Rapunzel's hair was very long.

loud

Loud means easy to hear. Loud is the same as noisy.

Cocky-Locky cried in a loud voice.

Cock-a-doodle-doo!

look (looked)

When you look, you use your eyes to watch something.

The Queen looked into the mirror.

love (loved)

If you love someone, you like them a lot.

Do you have a pet that you love?

lost

If you are lost, you do not know where you are.

Hansel and Gretel were lost in the dark wood.

low

If something is low, it is not high up.

The boy jumped over the low wall.

Mm

magic

Magic is strange or wonderful things or clever tricks. It can be hard to explain how magic works.

The rabbit came out of the hat by magic.

make (made)

When you make something, you put it together.

"I will make these shoes for the elves," said the shoemaker.

market

A market is a place where you can buy and sell things. A market is sometimes outdoors.

You can buy fruit and other foods at a market.

marry (married)

When a man and a woman marry, they become husband and wife.

"Let's marry!" said the prince.

mirror

A mirror is a special piece of glass. If you look in a mirror, you see yourself.

You use this mirror to look at your face.

midnight

Midnight is 12 o'clock at night.

The clock struck midnight.

mitten

A mitten is a kind of glove without fingers. Mittens keep your hands warm.

You need to wear mittens on a cold day.

milk

Milk is a white liquid that you drink. Mothers and some animals feed milk to their babies.

Baby Bear poured milk on his porridge.

money (monies)

Money is paper notes and coins. You use money when you buy something.

Money is made out of paper or metal.

monkey

A monkey is a furry animal that lives in trees. Monkeys are good at climbing.

This monkey has a long tail.

morning

Morning is the early part of the day. It ends at 12 o'clock in the middle of the day.

Snow White wakes up early each morning.

moon

The moon is high up in the sky. You can see the moon shining at night.

A full moon is big and round.

mountain

A mountain is a very big hill.

There is snow on the tops of these mountains.

mop

A mop is a long handle with soft material at one end. You use it to wash a floor.

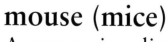

A mop makes it easier to wash the floor.

mouse (mice)

A mouse is a little, furry animal with a long tail. Mice have long, thin whiskers and sharp teeth.

Mice like to eat cheese.

mouth

Your mouth is a part of your face. You use your mouth to eat and to speak.

Inside the wolf's mouth are very big teeth!

mule

A mule is an animal that is half horse and half donkey.

A mule often pulls a cart.

mud

Mud is wet soil. Mud is sticky and dirty.

The old man and the old woman were covered in mud.

mushroom

A mushroom is a wild plant that grows in woods and fields. Some kinds of mushrooms are dangerous to eat.

A mushroom can be shaped like a tiny umbrella.

mug

A mug is a big cup.

Baby Bear drinks a mug of milk.

music

Music is the sound you make when you sing or play a musical instrument.

Rapunzel makes beautiful music.

N n

nail

A nail is a thin piece of metal with a point at one end. You can use nails to join pieces of wood.

The elves hammered the nails into the shoe.

A nail is also the hard part at the end of each of your fingers and toes.

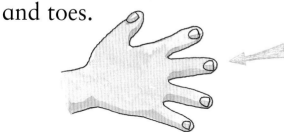

Are your nails long or short?

nasty

Someone who is nasty is not very kind to others.

The big, bad wolf was nasty.

needle

A needle is a thin piece of metal with a sharp point at one end and a hole at the other end for thread.

You sew with a needle.

nest
A nest is a place where birds, mice, and some other animals keep their babies.

There are six eggs in this nest.

nose
Your nose is on your face. You use your nose to breathe and to smell.

The gingerbread man jumped toward the fox's nose.

new
Something that is new is not old. It has just been made or bought.

The Emperor loved his new clothes.

number
A number tells you how many there are. You write a number as a word (two) or as a sign (2).

Match the numbers and words in this picture.

night
Night is the time when it is dark. Most people go to sleep at night.

Do you sleep with your teddy bear at night?

nut
A nut is a hard fruit from some kinds of trees. Many nuts have a hard shell on the outside.

Squirrels like to eat lots of nuts.

ocean

An ocean is a very big sea.

Very big ships sail across the ocean.

old

A person who is old was born a long time ago.

The old man had white hair.

offer (offered)

To offer is to hold out something for another person to take.

The old woman offered an apple to Snow White.

Old also means not new.

My old boots are not shiny like my new ones.

onion

An onion is a round vegetable with a strong smell and a strong taste.

You can use an onion when you cook soup.

outside

Something that is outside is not inside.

The wolf stood outside the house.

open (opened)

When you open a door, you can walk through it.

The prince opened the door.

over

If you go over something, you go across it and onto the other side.

The troll climbed over the side of the bridge.

orange

An orange is a round, juicy fruit. It has a thick skin that you take off.

Oranges are very good to eat.

owl

An owl is a bird with big eyes. Owls sleep in the day and hunt at night.

"Twit, twoo!" says the owl.

Pp

pair
A pair is two things that belong together.

The shoemaker found a pair of red shoes.

palace
A palace is the home of a king, a queen, a prince, or a princess.

The prince took Snow White to his palace.

parade
A parade is when people march in line so that other people can watch them.

The Emperor led the parade.

party (parties)

A party is when a group of people meet to enjoy a special time.

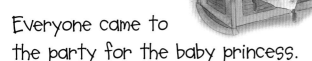

Everyone came to the party for the baby princess.

pig

A pig is an animal with a curly tail. Pigs live on farms.

Do you know a story about the three little pigs?

pebble

A pebble is a small, round stone.

Hansel followed the pebbles along the path.

plant (planted)

When you plant something, you put it in the ground so it grows.

The old man planted some turnip seeds.

peep (peeped)

To peep is to take a quick look at something.

Jack peeped out of the cupboard.

plate

A plate is a flat dish. You eat food from a plate.

Can you eat a big plate of spaghetti like this?

poison

Poison is something that can make you ill or kill you if you swallow it.

The queen put poison in the apple.

pot

A pot is a deep, round dish. It can hold food or water.

The little pig had a big pot of water.

poor

If you are poor, you have little or no money.

The shoemaker and his wife were very poor.

present

A present is something that you give to another person.

The present has a red ribbon around it.

porridge

Porridge is a hot food made from oats. You eat porridge for breakfast.

Mommy Bear made some porridge.

pretty

Someone or something that is pretty is lovely to look at.

Cinderella's dress turned into a pretty ball gown.

prince

A prince is the
son of a king
or a queen.

One day,
a prince
came riding by.

pull (pulled)

When you pull something, you
hold it and tug it toward you.

The old man and the
old woman tried
to pull the
enormous
turnip.

princess (princesses)

A princess is the daughter of a
king or a queen. The
wife of a prince is
also called a
princess.

The princess grew up to
be wise and kind.

pumpkin

A pumpkin is a big, round fruit.
It has a yellow or orange skin.

The fairy godmother
turned the pumpkin
into a coach.

promise (promised)

If you promise to do
something, you
are sure that
you will do it.

"I promised to go to
the Beast," said
Beauty.

push (pushed)

When you push
something, you
press against it
with your hands.

Gretel pushed
the witch into
the cooking pot.

quack

A quack is the sound that a duck makes.

"Quack, quack!" went the three ducklings.

quarrel (quarreled)

When you quarrel, you are angry. You quarrel because you do not agree with someone.

Do you sometimes quarrel with your friends?

quarter

If you cut something into four equal parts, each part is a quarter.

The pizza was cut into four quarters.

queen

A queen is a person who rules a country. A queen is also the wife of a king.

A queen often wears a crown on her head.

quiet

If someone is quiet, that person is not noisy.

A teacher sometimes says, "Sshh! Be quiet!"

question

You ask a question when you want to know something.

Do you ask lots of questions?

quilt

A quilt is a kind of bed cover.

There was a bright quilt on Grandma's bed.

quick

Quick means in a short time. If something is quick, it is very fast.

Cinderella was quick to run away.

quiver (quivered)

When you quiver, your body shakes.

Sometimes you quiver because you are cold.

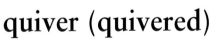

R r

rabbit

A rabbit has long ears and a little fur tail.
A rabbit can hop.

Rabbits have lots of babies.

rain

Rain is water that falls from the sky.
Rain falls as drops.

Do you like to walk in the rain?

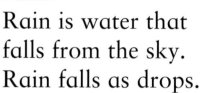

rainbow

A rainbow is an arch of colors in the sky. It happens when the sun shines through drops of rain.

A rainbow has lots of bright colors.

rake

A rake is a tool that you use in the garden. It has prongs and a long handle.

You use a rake to make the earth smooth.

ribbon

A ribbon is a thin piece of material. You can put a ribbon in your hair.

Sleeping Beauty had a ribbon in her hair.

rat

A rat is an animal that looks like a big mouse. It has a long tail.

Rats often live in pipes under the ground.

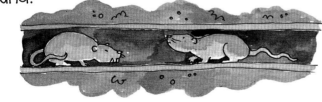

rice

Rice is a white or brown food that you cook. Rice comes from a plant that looks like grass.

Have you tried to eat rice with chopsticks?

read (read)

If you can read, you can say and understand words that are written down.

Do you like to read in bed?

rich

If you are rich, you have lots of money.

The rich woman had very fine clothes.

ride (rode)

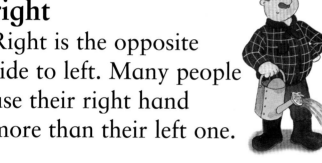

When you ride something, you sit on it while it moves along.

The prince rode on a brown horse.

rip (ripped)

To rip something is to tear it.

The man ripped the newspaper in half.

right

Right is the opposite side to left. Many people use their right hand more than their left one.

The old man holds the watering can in his right hand.

river

A river is moving water with land on each side. Most rivers flow into the sea.

A bridge went over the river.

ring

A ring is a circle of thin metal. You can wear a ring on your finger.

Beauty's sister had a shiny ring.

roar (roared)

To roar is to make a deep, loud sound.

The lion roared loudly.

rocket

A rocket is a big machine that flies into space.

The rocket lifts off the ground.

rose

A rose is a flower that smells sweet. Some rose bushes have thorns.

Beauty wanted a red rose.

rocking chair

A rocking chair moves backward and forward when you sit in it.

Daddy Bear had a big, blue rocking chair.

rug

A rug is a mat or a little carpet.

Goldilocks left her shoes on the rug.

root

The root of a plant is the part that grows under the ground.

This plant has many roots.

run (ran)

When you run, you move your legs and feet quickly.

The gingerbread man ran on and on.

S s

sad

When you are sad, you do not feel happy.

Cinderella is sad because she cannot go to the ball.

scare (scared)

To scare someone is to frighten them.

The ghost scared the cat.

salt

Salt is a fine, white powder. You put it on food to make it taste salty.

Mommy Bear put salt on the porridge.

school

You go to school to learn lots of things.

What is the name of your school?

scissors

Scissors have two sharp blades that are joined together. You cut things with scissors.

It's easy to cut paper with scissors.

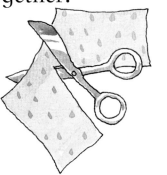

sell (sold)

If you sell something, you let someone have it for some money.

This man sells balloons.

scream (screamed)

When you scream, you cry out because you are frightened.

Little Red Riding Hood screamed!

servant

A servant is a person who works in someone's house for money.

The servant carried the Emperor's crown.

seed

A seed is a tiny part of a plant. A new plant will grow from a seed.

The old man had some turnip seeds.

sheep

A sheep is a farm animal. It has a woolly coat.

Sheep like to eat grass.

shirt

You wear a shirt on the top half of your body. It has buttons down the front.

This shirt has red, blue, and white stripes.

shout (shouted)

When you shout, you call out very loudly.

How loudly can you shout?

shoe

You wear a shoe on your foot. Shoes keep your feet warm and dry.

The red shoes were made of leather.

shut (shut)

To shut means to close. Something that is shut is not open.

The soldier shut his eyes and fell asleep.

shoemaker

A shoemaker is a person who makes shoes.

The shoemaker made two pairs of tiny shoes.

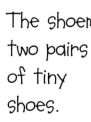

sing (sang)

When you sing, you make musical sounds with your voice.

Rapunzel used to sing each day.

single

If something is single, there is only one of it.

There is a single apple on this tree.

sleep (slept)

When you sleep, you close your eyes and rest.

The princess went to sleep in the castle.

skip (skipped)

When you skip, you hop from one foot to the other.

Goldilocks skipped with a jump rope.

smile (smiled)

When you smile, the corners of your mouth turn up. You smile to show you are happy.

Little Red Riding Hood smiles as she walks along.

sky (skies)

The sky is the space above the Earth. Airplanes fly in the sky.

At night, the moon and stars appear in the sky.

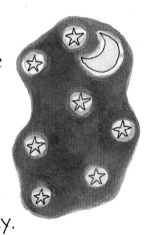

smoke

Smoke is the gray or black cloud from a fire.

Smoke comes out of a chimney.

snow

Snow is small, white pieces of frozen water. It falls from the sky when it is cold.

The snow falls on the snowman.

spell

A spell is a set of magic words to make something happen.

The wicked fairy cast a spell.

sock

You wear socks on your feet to keep them warm.

These blue socks have yellow spots.

spider

A spider is a small creature with eight legs. A spider can spin a web.

A spider catches flies in its web.

soup

Soup is a liquid that you eat with a spoon. You can make soup from vegetables.

The old woman made turnip soup.

spinning wheel

A spinning wheel is a machine that makes wool or cotton thread.

The princess touched the spinning wheel.

splash (splashed)

If you splash water, you make it fly up in the air.

The troll splashed into the water.

stable

A stable is a building where animals live.

This horse lives in a stable.

spoon

A spoon has a tiny bowl on the end of a handle. You eat ice cream with a spoon.

Daddy Bear's spoon is very big.

stair

A stair is a step inside a building or outside it. You can go up or down stairs.

The prince ran down the stairs.

spring

Spring is the time of year after winter. In the spring, the weather becomes warmer.

The ugly duckling waited for spring to come.

star

A star is a small, bright light that you see in the night sky.

There are millions of stars in the sky.

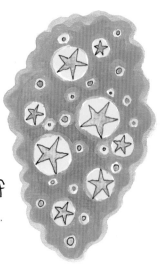

steal (stole)

If you steal, you take something that does not belong to you.

Beauty's father stole a rose from the Beast's garden.

straw

Straw is dried stems of corn or other grains.

The first little pig built a house of straw.

steam

Steam is a hot gas. Very hot food or boiling water gives off steam.

Steam came from the hot porridge.

A straw is also a thin tube made of paper or plastic. You drink through a straw.

Do you like to drink through a straw?

stick

A stick is a thin piece of wood.

The second little pig built a house of sticks.

strong

If you are strong, you can do jobs that need a lot of energy.

Jack uses his strong arms to carry the pails.

stupid

Someone who is stupid is not very clever.

"It was stupid to sell the cow for five beans!" said Jack's mother.

surprise

A surprise is something that happens when you do not expect it.

There was a big surprise in the box!

sugar

You add sugar to drinks and foods to make them taste sweet.

My mom puts sugar in her tea.

swan

A swan is a big, white bird with a long neck. Swans can swim and fly.

Three beautiful swans swam on the lake.

sun

The sun shines in the sky. It gives heat and light to the Earth.

You should wear a sunhat when the sun shines.

swim (swam)

When you swim, you use your legs and arms to move through water.

The fox began to swim across the river.

T t

tail

The tail is the part that grows out from the end of an animal's body.

The fox's tail had a white tip.

talk (talked)

When you talk, you speak words to another person.

The Emperor talked to his prime minister.

table

A table has legs and a flat top. You put things on a table.

The little pigs hid under the table.

taste (tasted)

When you taste something, you put it in your mouth to see what it is like.

Goldilocks tasted some porridge.

tea

Tea is a drink. You make it with hot water and dried tea leaves.

You can make tea in a teapot.

thief (thieves)

A thief is someone who steals things from others.

The thief climbed out of the window.

tear

A tear is a drop of water that falls from your eyes when you cry.

Rapunzel's tears fell on the prince.

thin

Something that is thin is not fat.

Hansel held out a thin chicken bone.

tell (told)

To tell is to speak the words of a story or some news to someone else.

My dad tells me a story every night at bedtime.

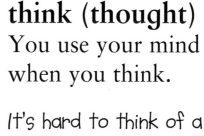

think (thought)

You use your mind when you think.

It's hard to think of a good idea.

thorn

A thorn is the sharp point that grows on some plants.

The prince fell onto some thorns.

thumb

Your thumb is a part of your hand. You have four fingers and one thumb on each hand.

Can you stick your thumbs up like this?

thread

Thread is a thin piece of cotton, silk, or wool. You use thread to sew and to make cloth.

Rumpelstiltskin spun the straw into gold thread.

tiny

Something that is tiny is very small.

Baby Bear had a tiny bowl.

throw (threw)

When you throw something, you make it move through the air.

How far can you throw a ball?

tooth (teeth)

A tooth is a hard, white part in your mouth. You use your teeth to bite your food.

The wolf had very big teeth.

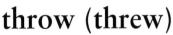

top

The top is the highest part of something.

The boy pats the top of his head.

toy

A toy is something that you play with.

What is your favorite toy?

tower

A tower is a very tall building.

There is a window near the top of this tower.

troll

A troll is a creature that you read about in some fairy tales.

The troll was very big and noisy.

town

A town is a busy place with lots of streets. It has many buildings, such as houses, shops, and offices.

Do you live in a town?

turnip

A turnip is a round vegetable. It grows under the ground.

Have you ever tasted a turnip?

Uu

ugly

A person who is ugly is not pretty to look at.

Cinderella had two ugly stepsisters.

under

If you are under something, you are not on top of it. Under means the same as below.

The pigs hid under the quilt.

umbrella

An umbrella keeps you dry in the rain. It is made of material that is stretched over a frame.

You hold an umbrella above your head.

upstairs

Upstairs is the top part of a house. You climb the stairs to go upstairs.

Goldilocks went upstairs.

valley

A valley is the low land between two hills.

There is a river in this valley.

vegetable

A vegetable is a plant that you can eat.

Which is your favorite vegetable?

van

A van is a small vehicle. People use vans to carry things from place to place.

The van brings lots of flowers.

vehicle

A vehicle is a machine that takes people or things from place to place.

Cars, bicycles, buses, and trains are vehicles.

walk (walked)

When you walk, you move by putting one foot in front of the other.

Hansel and Gretel walked back home.

wall

A wall is made from bricks or stones. It is built around a field, a garden, or a yard.

The garden wall is made of bricks.

wake (woke)

When you wake up, you are no longer asleep.

Goldilocks woke up.

wand

A wand is a special stick. People use a wand to make magic.

The fairy godmother had a magic wand.

warm

If something is warm,
it is not too hot
and not too cold.

Warm soup
is just right
to eat.

wave (waved)

When you wave something, you
move it backward and forward
or from side to side.

The fairy waved
her magic wand.

wash (washed)

When you wash
something, you
use soap and
water to make it
clean.

Do you wash your
face each morning?

wear (wore)

When you wear
clothes, you put
them on your
body.

Beauty likes to wear
her pretty pink dress.

watch (watched)

When you watch
something, you look
at it for a time.

The wolf watched
Little Red
Riding Hood.

weaver

A weaver makes cloth on a
special machine
called a loom.

The weavers
did not really
weave the
gold cloth.

wedding

A wedding is the time when a man and a woman get married.

Rapunzel and the prince had a lovely wedding.

window

A window is an opening in a wall or the side of a vehicle. A window is made of glass or plastic.

The three little pigs looked out of the window.

wheel

A wheel is round and it turns. Wheels help trains, cars, and bicycles to move.

This wheel is from a bicycle.

wing

A bird uses its wings when it flies. Airplanes also have wings.

The swan flapped its wings.

wicked

A wicked person is someone who is very bad.

The wicked queen looked in the mirror.

winter

Winter is the coldest time of the year. It is one of the four seasons.

Many trees lose their leaves in winter.

witch (witches)

In fairy tales, a witch is a woman who makes magic spells.

The witch was very angry.

woodcutter

A woodcutter is a person who cuts wood.

The woodcutter had a big ax.

wolf (wolves)

A wolf is a wild animal that looks like a large dog.

The wolf smiled at Little Red Riding Hood.

write (wrote)

When you write something, you make words on paper with a pen or pencil.

Do you write your name in your books?

wood

Lots of trees grow in a wood.

The three bears lived in a big wood.

wrong

If something is wrong, it is not right.

In the problem $5 + 4 = 8$, the answer is wrong.

$5 + 4 = 8$

X

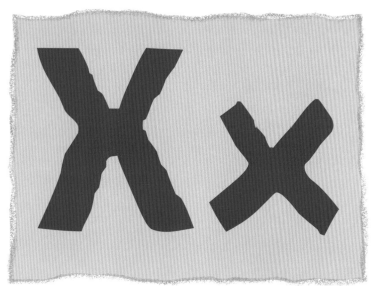

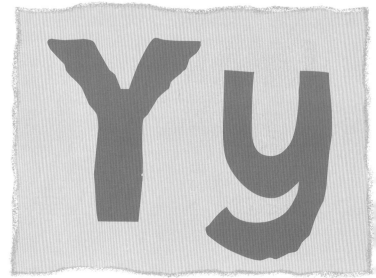

X-ray

An X-ray is a special photo of the inside of your body. Doctors look at X-rays to find out if any bones are broken.

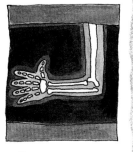

Which part of the body can you see in this X-ray?

yawn (yawned)

You yawn when you feel sleepy. When you yawn, you open your mouth wide.

The boy yawned at bedtime.

xylophone

A xylophone is a musical instrument. You make sounds by hitting it with hammers.

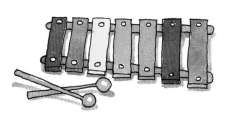

A xylophone is often painted in bright colors.

year

A year is an amount of time. There are 12 months, or 365 and a quarter days, in one year.

A calendar tells you what is happening during the year.

zebra

A zebra is an animal with stripes on its coat. A zebra looks like a horse.

Zebras live in Africa.

zipper

A zipper joins together two edges of material. You open a zipper by pulling it down.

The girl pulls the zipper on her sweater.

zero

Zero is the number 0. It is the same as nothing.

The answer to this problem is zero.

zoo

A zoo is a place where lots of wild animals live. People visit zoos to look at the animals.

Have you ever been to a zoo?

Numbers

1 one

2 two

3 three

4 four

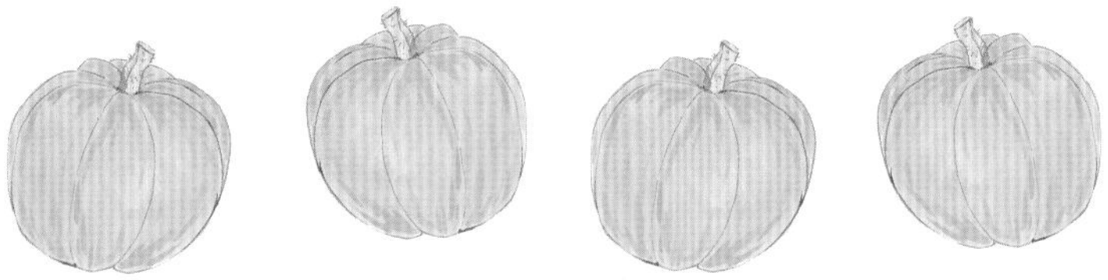

5 five

6 six

7 seven

8 eight

9 nine

10 ten

20 twenty	50 fifty	80 eighty
30 thirty	60 sixty	90 ninety
40 forty	70 seventy	100 hundred

Colors

a **red** apple

a **green** frog

a **blue** chair

a **black** pot

a **brown** goat

purple grapes

a **pink** dancer

an **orange** pumpkin

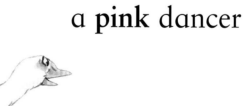

a **white** goose

three **yellow** ducklings

Opposites

good

bad

pretty

ugly

big

little

happy

sad

up

down

asleep

awake

93

Aa Bb Cc

Dd Ee

Ff Gg Hh

Ii Jj

Kk Ll Mm